CENGAGE Learning

Novels for Students, Volume 41

Project Editor: Sara Constantakis Rights Acquisition and Management: Mary Snell, Robyn Young Composition: Evi Abou-El-Seoud Manufacturing: Rhonda Dover

Imaging: John Watkins

Product Design: Pamela A. E. Galbreath, Jennifer Wahi Content Conversion: Katrina Coach Product Manager: Meggin Condino © 2013 Gale, Cengage Learning

ALL RIGHTS RESERVED. No part of this work covered by the copyright herein may be reproduced, transmitted, stored, or used in any form or by any means graphic, electronic, or mechanical, including but not limited to photocopying, recording, scanning, digitizing, taping, Web distribution, information networks, or information storage and retrieval systems, except as permitted under Section 107 or 108 of the 1976 United States Copyright Act, without the prior written permission of the publisher.

Since this page cannot legibly accommodate all copyright notices, the acknowledgments constitute an extension of the copyright notice.

For product information and technology assistance, contact us at **Gale Customer Support, 1-800-877-4253.**

For permission to use material from this text or product, submit all requests online at <u>www.cengage.com/permissions</u>.

Further permissions questions can be emailed to **permissionrequest@cengage.com** While every effort has been made to ensure the reliability of the information presented in this publication, Gale, a part of Cengage Learning, does not guarantee the accuracy of the data contained herein. Gale accepts no payment for listing; and inclusion in the publication of any organization, agency, institution, publication, service, or individual does not imply endorsement of the editors or publisher. Errors brought to the attention of the publisher and verified to the satisfaction of the publisher will be corrected in future editions.

Gale
27500 Drake Rd.
Farmington Hills, MI, 48331-3535

ISBN-13: 978-1-4144-9484-5
ISBN-10: 1-4144-9484-X
ISSN 1094-3552

This title is also available as an e-book.

ISBN-13: 978-1-4144-9270-4
ISBN-10: 1-4144-9270-7
Contact your Gale, a part of Cengage Learning sales representative for ordering information.

Printed in Mexico
1 2 3 4 5 6 7 16 15 14 13 12

Haroun and the Sea of Stories

Salman Rushdie 1990

Introduction

Salman Rushdie's *Haroun and the Sea of Stories* (1990) is a children's story that also has great appeal for adults. Not only is the novel a first-rate quest adventure but also provides a meditation on the importance of free speech and the value of storytelling. Often funny, sometimes sad, *Haroun and the Sea of Stories* concerns young Haroun Khalifa and his father, Sharif Khalifa, who is a master storyteller. When Sharif loses the ability to tell stories, partially because of his wife's betrayal and partially because of Haroun's insensitive remarks, Haroun sets out to help his father regain his craft. His journey takes him to the far side of the hidden moon Kahani and back.

Although the novel is light-hearted and filled with jokes, Rushdie wrote the book while in hiding. In 1988, Rushdie published *The Satanic Verses*, a novel that included a parody of the Prophet Muhammad, something considered blasphemous by conservative Muslims. In response to the publication, the Ayatollah Khomeini of Iran issued a *fatwa*, or death sentence, against Rushdie. The threat was real: others connected with the publication of the book were attacked and murdered. Consequently, Rushdie found himself living in a series of safe houses in England, separated from his son and unable to appear in public. *Haroun and the Sea of Stories* was Rushdie's first post-*fatwa* work, and many readers identify the villain of the story with the Ayatollah. *Haroun and the Sea of Stories* is an excellent introduction to the body of Rushdie's work. Whether read as political allegory, a fantastical quest adventure, or a coming-of-age story, the novel is both engaging and thought provoking.

Author Biography

Rushdie was born on June 19, 1947, in Bombay, India, to Anis Ahmed and Negin Rushdie. Although the family was from Kashmir, they moved to Bombay shortly before the writer's birth. When the subcontinent gained its independence from Britain in 1947, Muslims moved to the newly formed Muslim nation of Pakistan, while Hindus moved to an independent India. Despite this, Rushdie's Muslim family chose to stay in Bombay. Rushdie's education was in both English and Urdu.

Rushdie attended the Cathedral Boy's High School before continuing his education in England at the Rugby School, a prestigious private boys' school, and later at King's College, Cambridge. Upon graduation, he remained in England, where he worked as an actor for several years before turning to writing copy for an advertising agency to support himself. During this period, he wrote the novel *Grimus* and married Clarissa Luard in 1976. The couple had a son, Zafar, in 1980. Although *Grimus* was not a success, it set the stage for Rushdie to work on *Midnight's Children*, published in 1981 and dedicated to Zafar.

The novel was a huge success, garnering both critical praise and a wide readership. It won several important awards, including the Booker Prize and the James Tait Black Memorial Prize. It eventually went on to win the Best of the Booker awards in

2008. In addition, the book became a best seller, selling more than 250,000 copies within the first three years of publication. *Midnight's Children* was also quickly translated into more than twelve languages. Rushdie followed the publication with his novel *Shame* in 1983 and a nonfiction book, *The Jaguar Smile: A Nicaraguan Journey*, in 1987.

Rushdie's home life was less successful. In 1985, he separated from Luard and began an affair with the Australian author Robyn Davidson. By the time his divorce from Luard was finalized in 1987, he had broken off with Davidson and begun living with the American writer Marianne Wiggins, whom he married shortly thereafter.

On September 26, 1988, Rushdie's novel *The Satanic Verses* was published. This event set in motion a whole series of consequences that irrevocably altered Rushdie's life. The book was offensive to religious Muslims, and in 1988, India banned the book. From there, other Muslim countries followed suit, either requiring heavy censorship of the book or banning it all together. The most devastating blow, however, occurred on February 14, 1989. The Iranian Ayatollah Khomeini (famous in the United States for his role in the deposition of the Shah of Iran and the U.S. Embassy hostage crisis of 1979–1981), issued an edict called a *fatwa* against Rushdie and *The Satanic Verses*. He pronounced that Rushdie and all those involved in any way in the publication, printing, and selling of the book were sentenced to death.

Rushdie and his wife went into hiding

immediately, protected by the British Special Branch. They constantly moved locations, and it is likely that the stress placed on the couple by the danger and instability in their lives caused the breakup of the marriage by 1993. The *fatwa* continued for years, remaining in effect even after the death of Khomeini in 1989. The danger continued as well: in 1991, Rushdie's Japanese, Italian, Norwegian, and Turkish translators were all attacked, resulting in the death of Hitoshi Igarashi and the severe wounding of the others. According to Norbert Schürer, writing in *Salman Rushdie's "Midnight's Children,"* about sixty people died in all as a result of what came to be known as the Rushdie Affair.

It was under these circumstances, in hiding and separated from his son, Zafar, that Rushdie began writing *Haroun and the Sea of Stories*, a children's book he published in 1990. It is easy to read into the novel the themes of censorship and violence elicited by the *fatwa*.

Since 1990, Rushdie has published eleven more books and experienced two additional marriages and divorces. He emerged from hiding, cautiously at first, in 1993, and by 1995, was making public appearances again. In 1998, the Iranian government officially lifted the *fatwa*.

Rushdie has won most of the world's most prestigious literary awards. In 1993, he won the Booker of the Bookers for the best novel of all the Booker Award–winning novels published to date. In 2008, he repeated the honor by winning the Best of the Booker award. Both were for *Midnight's Children*. In 2007, Rushdie was knighted by Queen Elizabeth II for services to literature.

Rushdie's books are of great interest to scholars and students as well as to the general public. He continues to be one of the most important writers living in the twenty-first century.

Plot Summary

Chapter 1: The Shah of Blah

The story opens in the country of Alifbay. A boy named Haroun Khalifa lives in a sad city in that country. The city is "so ruinously sad that it had forgotten its name." Although the city is sad, Haroun lives happily with his father, Rashid, who laughs easily and his mother, Soraya, who sings beautifully. Rashid is a storyteller known by two names: to those who enjoy his stories, he is called Rashid the Ocean of Notions; to those who wish him ill, however, he is known as the Shah of Blah. Like many teenagers, Haroun is sometimes embarrassed by his father and his stories.

The Khalifa family's upstairs neighbors are Mr. Sengupta and his wife, Oneeta, a childless couple. Mr. Sengupta is very thin and whiny whileOneeta is large and generous. Mr. Sengupta is a minor city bureaucrat who loudly criticizes Rashid and his stories. "What's the use of stories that aren't even true?" he asks.

Media Adaptations

- Tim Supple and David Tushingham adapted *Haroun and the Sea of Stories* for the stage. The play was performed at the Royal National Theatre in London in 1998.

- An abridged audiobook version of the novel was read by Salman Rushdie and released by Penguin Audio in 1997.

- An opera based on *Haroun and the Sea of Stories* by Charles Wuorinen and libretto by James Fenton premiered at the New York City Opera in Fall 2004.

Rashid never pretends that his stories are anything other than fiction. Politicians often employ

Rashid to speak on their behalf because everyone loves Rashid's stories, despite the fact that Rashid always admits that everything he says is made up.

One day, Haroun comes home from school to find that his mother has run off with Mr. Sengupta. Rashid is completely heartbroken, as is Haroun, who now can no longer concentrate on anything for more than eleven minutes. Haroun is also bitter toward his father, believing that his mother has left because of him. Haroun throws Mr. Sengupta's words at his father: "What's the use of stories that aren't even true?" Haroun immediately regrets his unkind words, but the damage is done. Soon Rashid is unable to think of any more stories, and the politicians grow angry. They order Rashid to go to the Valley of K and redeem himself by telling stories or there will be real trouble for the Shah of Blah. Haroun feels terribly guilty over his father's situation and resolves to fix the problem himself.

Chapter 2: The Mail Coach

Because Rashid has fallen from favor, he and Haroun must travel to the Valley of K by mail bus. It is very crowded at the bus station, and it is difficult to find tickets. However, Haroun meets Mr. Butt, the mail coach driver, and hits it off with him. Mr. Butt puts them on the bus and asks if there is anything that Haroun wants. Haroun asks for a sunset view, thinking it will cheer his father. Butt then drives the bus at frightening speeds in order to reach the Valley of K in time for sunset. Everyone is terrified, and Haroun blames himself for his request. However, the sunset is truly magnificent and worth the terror. Rashid says that he thought that they were going to be killed. He uses the words "khattam-shud." When Haroun asks what that means, his father says,

> Khattam-Shud ... is the Arch-Enemy of all Stories, even of Language itself. He is the Prince of Silence and the Foe of Speech. And because everything ends, because dreams end, stories end, life ends, at the finish of everything we use his name.

As they enter the Valley of K, Haroun notices that someone has painted the words "Kosh-Mar" over the sign reading "Valley of K." Rashid shows himself to be an expert in ancient languages by recalling that, in the ancient tongue of Franj, the valley was once called Kosh-Mar or Kache-Mer. He also admits that, in the old tongue, that was the word for nightmare.

They are met by a shifty politician called Mr. Snooty Buttoo who takes them across Dull Lake. Haroun does not like Mr. Buttoo and is uncomfortable that there are so many soldiers needed to protect Mr. Buttoo. On Dull Lake, a terrible-smelling mist engulfs them.

Chapter 3: The Dull Lake

The mist is so thick and smells so bad that no one can stand it. Haroun calls it a Mist of Misery.

When the weather suddenly changes, he realizes that the lake is in Moody Land, a place where people's moods affect the weather. It is one of Rashid's most beloved stories. However, Rashid denies that they are in Moody Land, saying that it was only a story. Haroun tells his father that he must think happy thoughts, and when he does, the weather clears. Haroun no realizes that "the real world was full of magic, so magical worlds could easily be real."

They finally arrive at a luxurious houseboat that will be their accommodation for the night. In the library is a copy of *The Oceans of the Streams of Story*, a collection of tales. (This collection is, in fact, a real eleventh-century collection of Indian legends, folk tales, and fairy tales.)

Although the houseboat is comfortable, neither Haroun nor his father can sleep. Rashid is very depressed and anxious. They decide to switch bedrooms. Just as Haroun is finally dropping off to sleep, he is awakened by a Water Genie named Iff who has come to disconnect Rashid from his supply of story water from the great Story Sea. Haroun snatches Iff's Disconnector tool (an instrument something like a wrench) and refuses to return it until Iff takes him to Gup City on the hidden Moon Kahani to get the decision to disconnect Rashid reversed. Haroun now knows that his father's explanations about the Sea of Stories are true.

Chapter 4: An Iff and a Butt

The Genie tells Haroun to choose a bird and name it. The Genie has in his pocket tiny birds, and Haroun chooses a Hoopoe. Iff throws the tiny creature out the window, where it expands to a very large bird that looks a little like Butt the mail coach driver. Haroun thus calls the bird Butt the Hoopoe. Iff and Haroun jump on its back, and the bird flies away. Haroun discovers that Butt the Hoopoe is mechanical and that it can communicate with him telepathically.

They approach the Moon of Kahani and have a beautiful view of the Ocean of the Streams of Story, where they land. Iff tells Haroun to collect wish in a bottle, then drink it. It might save them the trouble of going to Gup City if Haroun can wish his father's troubles away. However, Haroun is not able to concentrate long enough to do so. He saves the wish water.

As they approach Gup City, Iff tells Haroun that the Ocean is being polluted and that many of the stories no longer make sense. He attributes the poisoning to Khattam-Shud, also known as the Cultmaster of Bezeban, from the dark side of Kahani.

Chapter 5: About Guppees and Chupwalas

In this chapter, Butt the Hoopoe explains the geography and details of Kahani. The rotation of Kahani has been brought under control by the Eggheads so that it is always light in Gup City and always dark in Chup City. As they continue on their journey across the ocean, they meet Mali, the Floating Gardener, and Bagha and Goopy, plentimaw fish. The plentimaw fish eat the stories in the ocean and then their digestive tracts make new stories out of the elements of the old. However, the pollution in the ocean is causing stories to be lost and damaged.

When they arrive in Gup City, the beauty of the palace and gardens entrances them. However, they soon discover that the Guppees are preparing for war with the Chupwalas.

King Chattergy and Prince Bolo, along with General Kitab and the Walrus, prepare to address the crowds gathered at the palace. Bolo reveals that his fiancée, the Princess Batcheat, has been kidnapped by the servants of the Cultmaster of Bezeban. They have sent messages to Khattam-Shud demanding her return and the cessation of the poisoning of the Ocean of the Streams of Story, but neither demand has been met. They declare war.

Suddenly there is a commotion, and a man with a sack over his head and his hands tied behind his back is led onto the balcony. He is identified as a captured spy. When the sack is removed, Haroun is startled to see his father, Rashid.

Chapter 6: The Spy's Story

Haroun pushes his way through the crowd and shouts at his father. The Guppees fall silent and Haroun tells them his father is not a spy at all.

Haroun and Iff are taken by a page named Blabbermouth. All the pages wear tunics with the texts of famous stories on them. When Haroun arrives in the Throne Room, he finds his father telling his story to Prince Bolo, General Kitab, and the Walrus. Rashid says that he transported himself to Gup in dream but made an error in calculation, ending up in the Twilight Strip between Gup and Chup. He reports that there are bad things happening there. A Cult of Muteness has developed, wherein followers of the Idol of Bezeban devote themselves to a lifetime of silence, sewing their lips together so that they cannot ever speak. In addition, Rashid saw Batcheat kidnapped while he was in the Twilight Strip. Rashid offers to lead the Gup army to the place where he saw the Chupwala army assembled. Haroun shouts that he will go with him.

Blabbermouth is appointed to take him back to his room. When the page's hat is dislodged, however, Haroun discovers that Blabbermouth is a girl, not a boy. Blabbermouth is beside herself and makes Haroun promise not to reveal her gender. Blabbermouth next entertains Haroun with a juggling act.

Chapter 7: Into the Twilight Strip

The next morning, Blabbermouth awakens Haroun to join the army of pages assembling in the Pleasure Garden. Haroun finds his father with Iff, and the Guppee forces prepare to depart. The members of the army all chatter away about the causes of the war and how it should be fought. Haroun takes issue with this, but Butt the Hoopoe argues that, once you give a people freedom of speech, you must expect them to use it.

As Haroun and the rest of the forces enter the Twilight Strip between Gup and Chup, his spirits fall. Butt tells him not to worry, that the Twilight Strip has this effect on everyone seeing it for the first time. The armies come ashore in Chup. Haroun, Blabbermouth, General Kitab, and Rashid begin to scout the area. They come across a warrior who is fighting his shadow in a silent, graceful dance. When the warrior becomes aware of them, he stops and gestures to them quickly. They do not understand him. The warrior then attempts to speak.

Chapter 8: Shadow Warriors

Bolo wants to fight the warrior, but Rashid quickly realizes that the gestures are a kind of language. Rashid is then able to communicate with the warrior, whose name is Mudra (a word that means sacred hand gestures in yoga). Mudra has left the army of the Cultmaster and is willing to assemble an army of other warriors and their shadows who will fight on the side of Gup against Khattam-Shud. The Warrior insists, however, that they must decide what to do first: save the Ocean from poison or save the Princess Batcheat. They decide to save Batcheat, but Haroun volunteers to go to the Old Zone to investigate the poisoning of the water. He volunteers because of his love for the stories his father tells. He says that he has only recently begun believing in the reality of the Ocean but now feels it is his duty to try to save it.

Thus, Haroun, Iff, Goopy, Bagha, and Mali with Butt the Hoopoe set off to the Southern Polar Ocean, where the Wellspring or Source of Stories is located. Before their journey is over, however, Goopy and Bagha cannot swim in the grossly polluted waters of the Southern Ocean. The rest of the companions continue. As they try to make their way through a weed-jungle, they are trapped by a Web of Night, a Chupwala weapon. The companions are taken prisoner.

Chapter 9: The Dark Ship

Iff breaks down in grief when he sees how poisoned the Ocean is here.

> We are the Guardians of the Ocean and we didn't guard it. ... The oldest stories ever made and look at them now. We let them rot, we abandoned them, long before this poisoning. We lost touch with our beginnings, with our roots, our Wellspring, our Source.

The group is surrounded by Chupwalas and led to a huge black boat, the flagship of Khattam-Shud. They are ordered on board. Iff manages to hand Haroun a small Bite-a-Light, a device that will give him two minutes of light if he bites down on it. Everything is in shadows and dark.

Finally, Haroun and Iff are confronted by Khattam-Shud himself, a "skinny, scrawny, measly, weaselly, snivelling clerical type." Haroun identifies him as Mr. Sengupta and begins to shout at him. The Cultmaster then changes shape and frightens all. Next he tells them he might as well show them what they came to see, since they will never be able to report back to the Guppees.

Chapter 10: Haroun's Wish

Khattam-Shud shows them vast machinery that manufactures poison. Since every story must be ruined in a different way, they have need of a great many poisons. He tells them about the Plug. He intends to plug the Wellspring of Stories itself, meaning that stories will cease.

At this minute, Mali's long tendrils begin to enter the ship. He quickly jumps on the ship's power generator, bringing the whole operation to a halt. Haroun bites on the Bite-a-Lite and blinds all the Chupwala soldiers who are used only to darkness. He dons a protective wet suit and dives into the ocean, catching a glimpse of the workers constructing the Plug. He remembers the wish water vial in his pocket and suddenly knows what to do. He returns to the surface and wishes that the Moon Kahani would spin normally so that both Gup and Chup would share equal hours of light and dark. Within eleven minutes, the light begins to pour down on Chup. The Chupwalas and the ship begin to melt. Haroun rescues Iff and Mali, and they all escape on Butt the Hoopoe. The poison has been destroyed and the Ocean will be able to heal.

Chapter 11: Princess Batcheat

Meanwhile, after Blabbermouth saves Bolo from a bomb, the armies of Gup who have been so chatty and honest fight together in a coordinated fashion and defeat the armies of Chup. Their silence has been their downfall because they were unable to communicate strategy. At the end of the battle, there is an earthquake caused by the spinning moon. A large statue of Bezeban crushes the real Khattam-Shud (the Khattam-Shud on the boat being the Shadow of the Cultmaster). As the Guppees enter Chup City, they hear Batcheat singing. They recover Batcheat, and peace is declared.

Haroun, however, is summoned to the office of the Walrus. His wish has destroyed all of the Eggheads' machinery, and he is being called to answer for himself.

Chapter 12: Was It the Walrus?

Haroun is terrified. He tries to persuade Iff and Mali to go with him, but they refuse. When he finally walks into the Walrus's office, he finds the Walrus, King Chattergy, Prince Bolo, Princess Batcheat, Blabbermouth, General Kitab, Iff, Mali, and Rashid, along with several others all assembled. He asks if he is in trouble, and the room erupts with laughter. They are pulling a joke on him. The real reason for the summons is so that he can be honored for his bravery and his saving of the Ocean of Stories. The Walrus tells him he can have anything he wants.

Haroun wants a happy ending but knows they cannot give it to him. The Walrus disagrees. He says that by a Process Too Complicated To Explain, they can make up a happy ending for him.

Butt the Hoopoe flies them back to Dull Lake, and when Haroun enters the houseboat, he immediately falls asleep. When he awakens, he finds his father sipping tea and talking about a strange dream. Mr. Buttoo arrives to take Rashid to his speaking engagement, and Haroun, wondering if the whole night was a dream, returns to his room. He finds a letter from Blabbermouth and signed by all his friends from Kahani telling him to return again. Enclosed is a tiny bird, Butt the Hoopoe, who will transport him wherever he wishes.

Rashid finds his voice again and announces that he will tell the story Haroun and the Sea of Stories. He begins with the first sentence of Rushdie's Haroun and the Sea of Stories. The story turns the people of the Valley of K against the corrupt Mr. Buttoo, and Haroun and Rashid return safely to their home. Everyone there is happy.

Haroun suddenly realizes that his wish has come true. The name of his city has been remembered. It is called Kahani. When Rashid and Haroun arrive at their apartment, Oneeta Sengupta tells them that they must hurry to celebrate. Soraya has returned home. When he awakens the next morning, he remembers that it is his birthday. He hears his mother singing in the living room.

Characters

Bagha

Bagha is a plentimaw fish, a type of fish with several mouths that consumes stories in the Ocean of the Stream of Stories. The stories are reassembled in the guts of the plentimaw fish and become new stories. Bagha is always with its partner, Goopy. The pair is named after two heroes from a movie by Satyajit Ray, according to Rushdie's glossary located at the end of the novel.

Princess Batcheat

Princess Batcheat is the daughter of King Chattergy and is engaged to Prince Bolo. Her terrible singing voice is an ongoing joke throughout the book, as are her unattractive nose and mouth. Her kidnapping sets in motion the war between Gup and Chup. According to Rushdie's glossary at the end of the novel, her name means "chit-chat."

Blabbermouth

Blabbermouth is a page in service to Prince Bolo, disguised as a boy. She is a talkative, intelligent, and courageous young woman. At first, she appears ill tempered with Haroun, but ultimately they become friends. She develops an infatuation and admiration for the warrior Mudra. Haroun has a crush on Blabbermouth and is happy when she kisses him.

Prince Bolo

Bolo is a prince in Gup who is engaged to the king's daughter Batcheat. He is a silly man, overdressed in the garb of royalty. He is not very smart and rarely judges his situation accurately. For example, at one point, he grants would-be assassins immunity against the advice of Blabbermouth and others. Only Blabbermouth's quick action saves him. He overrates his own courage and swordsmanship. On the other hand, although he is laughable, he loves Batcheat with all his heart despite her many shortcomings. Nor is he an evil character. Rather, he is a parody of a fairy-tale hero. According to Rushdie, his name means "Speak!"

Mr. Butt

Mr. Butt is the mail coach driver. He and Haroun become friends early in the book, and he promises him that Haroun and his father will see a beautiful sunset over the Valley of K. To do so, however, he drives excessively fast and recklessly. He is Butt the Hoopoe's counterpart in the "real" world.

Butt the Hoopoe

Butt the Hoopoe is a large mechanical bird

who can communicate with Haroun telepathically. He provides transportation from Earth to Kahani for Haroun and Iff. He resembles the mail coach driver in both appearance and speech patterns.

Snooty Buttoo

Snooty Buttoo is a corrupt politician who hires Rashid to speak on his behalf, in order to win reelection. He is arrogant and cruel and does not deserve reelection. While in the Valley of K, Rashid and Haroun stay on a houseboat that Snooty Buttoo provides. When Rashid returns from Kahani, the story he tells turns the people against Buttoo, and Buttoo leaves the Valley of K, never to be heard from again.

King Chattergy

King Chattergy is Batcheat's father and the figurehead ruler of Gup.

The Eggheads

The Eggheads are a group of scientists and engineers who have devised all of the Processes Too Complicated to Explain (P2C2E). They are responsible for altering Kahani's orbit so that Gup is always in daylight and Chup is always in darkness. They can also create happy endings for stories, and they have developed a method for distributing story water across the face of the Earth.

Goopy

Goopy is a plentimaw fish, a type of fish with several mouths who consume stories in the Ocean of the Stream of Stories. The stories are reassembled in the guts of the plentimaw fish and become new stories. Goopy is always with its partner, Bagha. The pair is named after two heroes from a movie by Satyajit Ray, according to Rushdie's glossary located at the end of the novel.

Iff

Iff is a Water Genie dispatched to disconnect Rashid from the supply of water coming from the Stream of Stories. When Haroun takes his Disconnector from him, he is obliged to take Haroun to the Moon Kahani and Gup City to plead Rashid's case with the Walrus. Iff's pattern of speech includes many clichés and synonyms. Although at first annoyed with Haroun for the theft of his Disconnector, Iff proves to be a boon companion.

Haroun Khalifa

Haroun is the protagonist of *Haroun and the Sea of Stories*. While his age is not given, events in the story imply that he is probably twelve or thirteen. That is, he is young enough to still be in school and live at home, but also old enough to be embarrassed by his father and interested in girls. Haroun's parents believe that he is an exceptional child, although he refuses to believe it. Nonetheless, the events of the story prove that his parents' assessment is not wrong. He is compassionate and responsible, feeling deeply for the trouble his words cause his father. He takes it upon himself to try to solve his father's problem, since he feels responsible for having caused it. Haroun is also resourceful. He quickly snatches the Water Genie's Disconnector tool, in order to preserve his father's access to stories as well as to give him an edge in negotiating with Iff to take him to Gup City. Finally, Haroun is a very brave boy. Although it is dangerous, he volunteers to go to the Old Zone to spy on Khattam-Shud, and while there, he escapes from capture, figures out a way to win the war, and saves his friends. Haroun grows over the course of the story and realizes that all that really matters to him is that his father and mother are happy with each other again.

Rashid Khalifa

Rashid is Haroun's father, variously known as the Ocean of Notions and the Shah of Blah for his talent in creating stories on the spot. He earns his living as a storyteller, often working for politicians who want him to help them win reelection. After a period of being completely absorbed in his career, he loses his wife to another man and is heartbroken. His heartbreak results in his being unable to tell stories. Rashid is a kind father who loves his son and his wife. In addition, he is a brave man himself. On Kahani, he defends himself against charges of spying and subsequently leads the Guppee armies to the location of the Chupwala tents. He regains his ability to tell stories after his visit to Kahani. More importantly, the stories he tells after he returns from Kahani no longer support corrupt politicians but put them in their places. Thus, the novel allows not only Haroun to mature and grow, it also allows Rashid to become a better father, husband, and storyteller.

Soraya Khalifa

Soraya is Haroun's mother and Rashid's wife. Although initially happy in the story, she grows weary of Rashid's stories over the years. She stops singing and then runs away with Mr. Sengupta. At the end of the story, she realizes her error and returns to the family and resumes singing in the living room.

Khattum-Shud

Khattum-Shud is the evil villain of the novel. He is also referred to as the Cultmaster of Bezaban. (Bezaban, according to Rushdie, means "Without-a-Tongue.") Khattum-Shud hates stories and words and wants silence. He is the enemy of free speech and the ruler of Chup. He has started a religion in which practitioners must sew their lips together to prevent them from speaking. His "real-world" counterpart is Mr. Sengupta. According to Rushdie's glossary, his name means "completely finished" or "over and done with."

General Kitab

General Kitab is the leader of the Guppee army. He is a good man and a strong leader who supports the rights of his troops to question his authority and debate strategy. He is frequently embarrassed by Prince Bolo's over-the-top and inappropriate responses to battle situations and diplomatic negotiations.

Mali

Mali is a floating gardener, a species made up of vines and water plants. His major task is to make sure stories do not become too complicated or knotted up. He does this by cutting away weeds and straightening out root systems. He is a boon companion to Haroun and is responsible for saving the day when Haroun is held captive by Khattam-Shud.

Mudra

Mudra is a warrior who defected from Khattam-Shud's army. He has learned how to disconnect his shadow from himself and has trained the entire army to do so. He and his shadow practice martial arts with each other. Mudra has difficulty speaking with his voice but is eloquent in an ancient language of gestures. He and his fellow warriors and shadows join the Gup forces in their war against the Chupwalas. According to Rushdie's glossary, Mudra "speaks Abhinaya, the Language of Gesture" used in classical Indian dance. Rushdie continues, "a 'mudra' is any one of the gestures that make up the language."

Mr. Sengupta

Mr. Sengupta is the Khalifas' upstairs neighbor. He is a skinny, whiny, minor civil servant who hates stories and has an eye for Soraya. He persuades her to run away with him, setting the rest of the events of the story in motion. He is the "real-world" counterpart of Khattam-Shud.

Oneeta Sengupta

Oneeta Sengupta is Mr. Sengupta's wife. She is a large, compassionate woman who loves Haroun as a son. Her husband's desertion causes her both embarrassment and pain.

The Walrus

The Walrus is the head of the Eggheads, so called because of his mustache.

Themes

Storytelling

Janet Mason Ellerby, writing in Lion and the Unicorn, identifies storytelling as an important theme in Haroun and the Sea of Stories. She writes, "Rushdie addresses the serious theme of storytelling and its critical link to cultural emancipation within his own rollicking story of a boy's fabulous adventures."

Early in the novel, Mr. Sengupta says, "What are all these stories? Life is not a storybook or joke shop. All this fun will come to no good. What's the use of stories that aren't even true?" After Soraya leaves the family and Rashid is heartbroken, Haroun shouts the same question at his father, blaming him for his mother's unhappiness. The remaining pages of the novel attempt to answer that very question.

Topics for Further Study

- With a group of your classmates, choose several scenes from *Haroun and the Sea of Stories* that seem particularly vivid to you. Using paints, pastels, and other media, create illustrations for the book. Mount the exhibit and invite others in your school to view your creation.

- Read Isabelle Allende's young-adult novel *City of the Beasts* (2002). The story features two young people who travel to the magical world of the Amazon. Analyze the novel as a coming-of-age story and write an essay in which you compare and contrast what Haroun has learned with what the main characters of *City of the Beasts* have learned.

- Using the Internet and your school library, research the region known as Kashmir. Why has this region been so troubled since 1947? Using software such as Glogster, create a poster that embeds important issues, illustrations, news reports, and other relevant materials so that others in your class can learn about this area of the world.

- With a group of your classmates,

write a play adaptation of *Haroun and the Sea of Stories*. Record your presentation of your play and post to YouTube for others to view.

- Read *The Annotated Alice: The Definitive Edition* by Lewis Carroll, with introduction and notes by Martin Gardner. This is a fully annotated edition, revealing all of Carroll's political, historical, philosophical, and literary allusions. Now, return to *Haroun and the Sea of Stories*. Prepare similar annotations for several chapters of *Haroun*. If you are able, work with others so that you can create a fully annotated version of the novel.

- With a small group, research the Ayatollah Khomeini, the *fatwa*, and the Rushdie Affair. Write a news script and present a newscast reporting on the incident.

Haroun discovers on his journey first to the Valley of K, later to Kahani, and finally back to his hometown again, that stories carry great power. Without stories, all is silence. Stories connect the past to the present and the present to the future. They carry in them the bits and pieces of all human experience. Through the creative act of storytelling, humans recreate themselves.

Likewise, as Haroun makes his journey, he discovers that the stories his father has told him since he was a child are true, although they seem fantastic to him. He learns that there really is a Sea of Stories and that the archenemy Khattam-Shud, the enemy of all language, exists. Rushdie's point seems to be that fiction has a purpose and that stories carry truths even when, paradoxically, they are not true.

Throughout the novel, Rushdie also reiterates his philosophy of storytelling. No story is new; all stories are made up of bits and pieces of other stories. "Any story worth its salt," exclaims Butt the Hoopee, as Haroun and his companions travel to Gup City, "can handle a little shaking up!" Iff the Water Genie expands on this comment. He tells Haroun, "Nothing comes from nothing, Thieflet; no story comes from nowhere; new stories are born from old—it is the new combinations that make them new." Thus, for Rushdie, every act of storytelling is simultaneously one of destruction and then reconstruction. Storytelling is recycling; the new story is created out of old elements.

Finally, storytelling serves yet another purpose in the novel. David Appelbaum, writing in a review appearing in Parabola tells the reader that "story telling is the antidote for sadness in Salman Rushdie's delightful new novel." Stories allow humans to escape the drudgery of their daily lives, experience adventures they could not in real life, and feel emotions absent in their humdrum existences. Stories not only educate their listeners, they also make them happy.

Language

Throughout *Haroun and the Sea of Stories*, Rushdie plays with language, using puns, onomatopoeia, allusion, and other figures of speech. The use of these techniques in the novel runs deeper than mere stylistics, however. The subject of language serves as a serious thematic concern for Rushdie. In an interview with Davia Nelson, Rushdie suggests that his experience with the *fatwa* during the writing of *Haroun* deeply affected how he felt about language. He states, "I guess [I] had become involved myself in a sort of war between language and silence—I suddenly understood the meaning of the story that I hadn't previously understood."

The purpose of the fatwa issued against Rushdie was to shut him up, permanently. By killing Rushdie, the Ayatollah would put an end not only to the storyteller but also to the stories. Indeed, during the early days of the fatwa, Rushdie was in deep hiding and did not appear to his audiences. Gradually, this changed. Rushdie chose to write Haroun and the Sea of Stories in retaliation.

It is not surprising that the arch villain of the novel is Khattam-Shud, the Prince of Silence and the Foe of Speech. Many scholars agree that this villain is a stand-in for Khomeini. Just as Khattam-Shud wants to stop all stories, Khomeini wanted to censor and silence any who disagreed with him and his belief system.

Thus, for Rushdie, hiding from death, the importance of being able to speak and tell stories became ever clearer. When the voice is silenced, everything ends. As he writes in Haroun, "Because dreams end, stories end, life ends, at the finish of everything we use his name. 'It's finished,' we tell one another, 'it's over. Khattam-Shud: The End.'" For Rushdie, the end of the language is the end of everything.

Style

Magical Realism

One of the most important styles found in late twentieth-and early twenty-first-century literature and art is magical realism (sometimes referred to as "magic realism.") While the work might seem realistic on the surface, fantasy, myth, magic, the supernatural, and dreams invade and at times coopt the work. Magical realism had its earliest articulations in the works of South American writers; perhaps the best-known magical realist in the world is Colombian writer Gabriel García Márquez, who was in turn influenced by Argentine writer Jorge Luis Borges. Other important writers of magical realism include Italian writer Italo Calvino, English writer John Fowles, and German writer Günter Grass.

In *Haroun and the Sea of the Stories*, Rushdie clearly draws on magical realism to create his story. As the novel opens, Haroun lives in a realistic household consisting of his father, his mother, and his upstairs neighbors. Although the city where Haroun lives sounds like many industrial cities, the element of magical realism enters in quickly: "In the north of the sad city stood mighty factories in which (so I'm told) sadness was actually manufactured, packaged, and sent all over the world."

The truly magical part of *Haroun*, however, happens after Haroun and his father travel to the Valley of K and are taken to a houseboat where they are to spend the night. In the middle of the night, Haroun is awakened by a supernatural being, Iff the Water Genie. While Iff is obviously magical, he is also realistic, behaving like the plumber he is, come to turn off the water. The combination of the realistic elements with the purely fantastical serves to make the scene more humorous and also more meaningful.

Further, when Haroun travels to the moon Kahani and experiences his amazing adventures, readers might wonder if all of the action is part of a fantastic dream, similar to the one experienced by Dorothy in *The Wizard of Oz*. However, like Dorothy, Haroun finds evidence after his return that the journey was real, regardless of how magical it seemed. Haroun's return to his home signals the return to the so-called real; however, his mother's return and the return of the family unit are by far the most magical events Haroun could ever have hoped for. Perhaps Haroun's most important lesson is the one he learns on his journey: "He knew what he knew: that the real world was full of magic, so magical worlds could easily be real."

The Journey of the Hero

In creating *Haroun and the Sea of Stories*, Rushdie drew on one of the oldest story devices known, the journey of the hero. Since humans have begun telling and recording stories, the heroic journey has been the core of the repertoire. Stories such as *The Epic of Gilgamesh, The Iliad, The Odyssey*, and Beowulf all feature a young hero who leaves home, travels far, learns much, shares his adventures with boon companions, and returns home, a wiser and more experienced person. Joseph Campbell, in his groundbreaking 1949 book *The Hero with a Thousand Faces*, detailed the stages and characteristics of the heroic journey. Susanna Schrobsdorff, writing in *Time*, comments, "Campbell drew from ancient allegories in dozens of cultures and codified [them] into one rollicking human epic, a universal saga that he referred to as the monomyth."

One of the best-known heroic journey stories in contemporary culture is that of George Lucas's *Star Wars*. Likewise, the *Harry Potter* novels follow Campbell's descriptions of the hero and his or her journey.

Haroun demonstrates many of the stages described by Campbell. The heroic quest always starts with a challenge or call to the journey, usually because of some important need or desire. In the case of Haroun, he begins his journey because he feels that he must help his father. Heroes often also receive supernatural help. Haroun is helped by Iff the Water Genie and a host of other supernaturally talented allies. Heroes often find themselves in a dark, difficult place where it is uncertain whether they will survive. For Haroun, this comes when he is on board ship with Khattam-Shud. Sometimes

Rushdie's use of the heroic journey is deliberately satirical. For example, heroes generally run into some sort of goddess who helps them on their way. Haroun runs into Blabbermouth, a chatty girl disguised as a boy, serving as a Guppee page. Many heroic stories include reconciliation with a father figure. In the novel, Haroun first denigrates his father and then later comes to admire and respect him. Indeed, the impetus for his journey is to atone for his transgression against his father, a transgression that takes away his father's gift of storytelling.

Finally, the heroic journey story ends with the hero returning home. Through his or her journey, he or she has grown in significant and important ways. Haroun demonstrates his growth through the maturity of his wish, that his family be reunited. As a result of his journey, his town is no longer sad. Everyone benefits from his contribution, and he has proved himself to be, though a young boy, heroic in every sense.

Historical Context

Kashmir

In both his fiction and nonfiction, Rushdie often refers to Kashmir, a highly contested area located on the northern border of India and the northeast border of Pakistan. In *Haroun and the Sea of Stories*, several locations can be identified with Kashmir, including The Valley of K, also known as Kache-Mer and Kosh-Mar. The glossary written by Rushdie and included in the text of *Haroun and the Sea of Stories* also notes that the fictional Dull Lake is named for Dal Lake in Kashmir. Rushdie's association with Kashmir runs deep; his family lived in Kashmir until just before Rushdie's birth in 1947, and Rushdie continues to comment on the situation in the beleaguered region. An article in the September 24, 2001, issue of the British newspaper the *Telegraph* provides a brief history of the region's conflicts, shedding light on Rushdie's ongoing fascination with Kashmir.

In 1947, India gained independence from Britain. Part of the agreement included the creation of the state of Pakistan. The partition of the Indian subcontinent was largely along religious lines, with Pakistan becoming a Muslim state and India becoming a Hindu one, based on the religious affiliation of the majority of the population in each area. The partition was not neat, however; according to the *Telegraph*, there were some 650 princely states, including Kashmir, within the new countries. The states were forced to join one or the other of the new countries, depending on their location. Located on the border of both India and Pakistan, Kashmir had a choice of whether to join with India or Pakistan. The choice was not peaceful. In 1947 and 1948, Indian and Pakistani armed forces fought a war over the region.

In 1948, the United Nations intervened and asked both warring parties to remove their troops in anticipation of a vote by the inhabitants of Kashmir as to their preference. Pakistan refused to stop fighting. In 1949, the countries observed a cease-fire. At this point, about 65 percent of the territory was held by India, with the remaining 35 percent held by Pakistan; the Kashmir Valley was claimed by both countries, according to an August 11, 2011, article appearing in the *New York Times*.

Since 1949, India and Pakistan have engaged in all-out war over Kashmir several times. One of the most serious outbreaks of fighting began with an insurgency of Kashmiris in 1989, eventually resulting in the deaths of more than 60,000 people. The *New York Times* further reports that the insurgency was "partly fueled by training, weapons, and cash from Pakistan," which wanted to use the Kashmiri independence movement to wrest control of the region from India. During this period, thousands of people, mostly young Kashmiri men, went missing. (In August 2011, mass graves containing the bodies of more than two thousand people were found in Kashmir.)

Compare & Contrast

- **1990s**: In Kashmir, an independence movement, aided by funding from Pakistan, continues an insurgency resulting in the deaths of many people.
  Today: Although in a period of relative peace, the situation in Kashmir is still volatile. A mass grave with thousands of bodies from the 1990s is uncovered in 2011.

- **1990s**: Rushdie is in hiding after the Ayatollah Khomeini issues an edict called a *fatwa*, encouraging all Muslims to murder Rushdie in response to the publication of his book *The Satanic Verses*.
  Today: The *fatwa* is lifted, and Rushdie has come out of hiding. He is still, however, considered to be in some danger from radical Islamists who do not recognize the lifting of the *fatwa*.

- **1990s**: Rushdie is under the protection of the British government's Special Branch security teams in response to the *fatwa*.
  Today: Rushdie is awarded a

knighthood by Queen Elizabeth II for his contributions to literature. The event touches off protests and riots among Muslims.

- **1990s**: Rushdie wins the Booker of the Bookers award for *Midnight's Children* in 1993. The award signifies that this book is considered the best among all of the books awarded the Booker Prize since the award's inception.

  Today: By public vote, *Midnight's Children* wins the Best of the Booker award, commemorating the prize's fortieth anniversary.

It was against this backdrop of intrigue, violence, and contested territory that Rushdie wrote *Haroun and the Sea of Stories*. The conflict between India and Pakistan over the Kashmir Valley clearly parallels the conflict between the fictional Guppees and the Chupwallas in the novel.

The Ayatollah Khomeini and the Fatwa

Ruhollah Khomeini was an Iranian religious scholar, born in 1900, who achieved the title of "ayatollah" in the 1920s, according to the *BBC History* website. An *ayatollah* is a high-ranking Shiite Muslim scholar. In the 1960s, Khomeini became politically active in opposing the rule of the Shah of Iran, whose regime was pro-Western. Khomeini pushed for a return to conservative Islam and for Iran to be governed by Islamic law. In 1962, the Shah had Khomeini arrested, immediately making him a hero to those who opposed the Shah. Released into exile in 1964, Khomeini continued to agitate from abroad for the Shah's overthrow.

In 1979, Khomeini and his party were successful in bringing down the Shah. Khomeini returned to Iran and was elected the country's religious and political leader. He maintained his anti-American, anti-Western stance, and under his influence, radical students stormed the U.S. Embassy in Tehran on November 4, 1979, taking a number of Americans hostage. The Americans were held for over a year.

In September 1988, Rushdie's *The Satanic Verses* was published in Britain. Reviewers were immediately concerned about the potential Muslim backlash against the novel because Muslims found the content of the book highly offensive. By early October, India had banned the book and Rushdie began receiving death threats. The furor continued over the following months, leading to riots and book burnings across the world, even in England. Finally, on February 14, 1989, Khomeini, speaking as the ruler of Iran and the religious head of all Shiite Muslims, issued a *fatwa* against Rushdie. Khomeini called on Muslims around the world to execute all who were involved in the writing, publication, and distribution of *The Satanic Verses*.

An Iranian religious foundation offered a $1-million USD reward for anyone who murdered Rushdie.

Khomeini died in June 1989 without revoking the *fatwa*. As a result, Rushdie remained in hiding under close protection for many years, including the years during which he wrote *Haroun and the Sea of Stories*. Most critics agree that the arch villain Khattam-Shud is a caricature of Khomeini.

Critical Overview

When *Haroun and the Sea of Stories* was published in 1990, reviewers responded very favorably. Rushdie wrote the book under extraordinary circumstances. The Ayatollah Khomeini of Iran had issued a sentence of death (known as a *fatwa*) on Rushdie in response to the 1988 publication of *The Satanic Verses*. Rushdie immediately went into hiding under stiff protective custody. He moved house constantly and was separated from his family, particularly his son, most of the time. The knowledge of these circumstances seems to have affected many reviewers. Indeed, most early reviews focus on the parallels between the *fatwa* and Rushdie's story. Edward Blishen, for example, writing in *New Statesman and Society*, asserts, "It's a tale that springs clearly enough out of the predicament of a writer who, by elaborate chance, has taken upon his shoulders the whole implicit peril of the storyteller's trade." Likewise, Sybil Steinberg, writing in *Publishers Weekly*, references the "unprecedented controversy generated by *The Satanic Verses*," noting that, in *Haroun and the Sea of Stories*, "Rushdie offers as eloquent a defense of art as any Renaissance treatise."

At the same time, many critics agree with Denis Donoghue, who, in an early review appearing in the *New Republic*, suggests, "There is something for everybody in *Haroun and the Sea of Stories*."

Both adults and children could enjoy the story, the critics seem to agree. For example, Rosalía Baena, writing in *Journal of Commonwealth Literature*, reads *Haroun and the Sea of Stories* as a work aimed at a "double audience: on the one hand a young reader can enjoy the story of Haroun and his father Rashid." Baena continues, "On the other hand, an adult reader and a literary critic perceive at least two other layers of meaning, at a political and a metafictional level."

In a slightly later study, James Harrison, writing in his *Salman Rushdie* (1992), comments on the similarity between Rushdie's situation and the plot of *Haroun*, noting, however, that the book plays with language as well as providing political commentary. Moreover, according to Harrison, Rushdie's work does not fall into the trap of being overly preachy and didactic:

> Never, as one reads the book, does such potential didacticism displace, or overshadow, or even diminish the pleasure one derives from the playful inventiveness of the fantasy and the sheer vigor and "jump" of the story.

Indeed, many scholars comment on the allegorical nature of *Haroun*. Eva König, for example, writing in *International Fiction Review*, asserts, "The interpretation of the novel as an allegory about democratic and artistic freedom is favored in the Anglocentric world." König, however, finds another reading more satisfying. Though she believes that the allegorical reading "in the shadow of the *fatwa*" reflects the construction of the story, she also argues that Rushdie "simultaneously sets up and deconstructs such a simple allegorical interpretation." For König, the novel's importance is as a commentary on colonialism:

> It can be argued that this novel is also about an ex-colony waking up to a new understanding of the postcolonial condition. ... Seen in this light, *Haroun and the Sea of Stories*, a 'minor' novel according to some critics, takes its rightful place among Rushdie's others works dealing with the postcolonial condition.

Likewise, Patricia Merivale, writing in *ARIEL*, notes that *Haroun* is "strikingly postcolonial: it subverts, or at least gives a little twist to, an eclectic amalgam of colonial 'classical' Children's Literature."

Other scholars provide various additional commentaries. Suchismita Sen, for one, focuses on the act of communication in *Haroun and the Sea of Stories*: "In Haroun's story, Rushdie provides a child's-eye view of the intricate and often intangible nature of interpersonal communication." Daniel Roberts, writing in *ARIEL*, suggests that *Haroun and the Sea of Stories* "makes sophisticated use of a number of literary allusions from various Romantic-period texts." Roberts also argues that the use of these allusions creates a stronger political statement, particularly with regard to Kashmir.

In an innovative and interesting article, Aron R. Aji, writing in *Contemporary Literature*, looks at the "legacy of Islam" in the narrative details of *Haroun*. He raises two important questions concerning the text: first, he wonders if there is a "kinship" between stories and religion, since both stories and religion speak so fully to what it means to be human. Second, he asks whether this kinship can "serve as grounds for reconciliation between the Islamic faith and the pluralistic cultural traditions of its community." Aji answers both questions with a resounding "yes."

Finally, David Applebaum, writing in *Parabola*, finds that *Haroun and the Sea of Stories* shares many features with *The Arabian Nights*. He also reads the story of young Haroun as a classic story of a heroic journey.

What Do I Read Next?

- Lewis Carroll's children's classics, *Alice's Adventures in Wonderland* and *Through the Looking Glass*, first published in 1865 and 1871, bear similarities to *Haroun and the Sea of Stories* in their use of puns, satire, fantastic occurrences, and sly comments on contemporary politics. A particularly interesting one-volume edition of the two books is *The Annotated Alice* (2000), with introduction and notes by Martin Gardner.

- Rushdie draws heavily on the famous collection of stories *One Thousand and One Arabian Nights* for source material for *Haroun and the Sea of Stories*. Geraldine McCaughrean provides a one-volume selection of the stories designed for readers ten and up in *One Thousand and One Arabian Nights* (Oxford Story Collections), published in 2000.

- In 2002, Chilean writer Isabelle Allende published the young-adult novel *City of the Beasts*. The novel tells the tale of fifteen-year-old Alexander Cold and twelve-year-old Nadia Santos, who journey to the magical world of the Amazon with a party of people, including

Alexander's grandmother, a doctor, a guide, a soldier, and native peoples looking for the mythical creature known as The Beast.

- *Luka and the Fire of Life* by Salman Rushdie, published in 2010, is a sequel to *Haroun and the Sea of Stories*. The novel features Luka, Haroun's younger brother, who must embark on a dangerous journey to the Magic World in order to save his father's life.

- *Islam in the World*, 3rd edition (2006), by Malese Ruthven provides a lucid overview of the major issues surround Islam in the world today. In this edition, the author covers the Rushdie Affair, considering both the events and the consequences of the publication of *The Satanic Verses*.

- British writer Jasper Fforde has created a fantastic alternate reality in his series of "Thursday Next" novels. In these books, literary detective Thursday Next takes on cases that protect characters and stories of famous books by entering the Book World, the place where all stories originate. *The Well of Lost Plots* (2003) offers the best description of the Book World.

Sources

Abrams, M. H., "Allusions," in *A Glossary of Literary Terms*, 6th ed., Harcourt Brace Jovanovich, 1993, pp. 8–9.

Aji, Aron R., "'All Names Mean Something': Salman Rushdie's *Haroun* and the Legacy of Islam," *in Contemporary Literature*, Vol. 36, No. 1, Spring 1995, pp. 103–29.

Applebaum, David, Review of *Haroun and the Sea of Stories*, in *Parabola*, Vol. 16, No. 2, May 1991, pp. 126–32.

"Ayatollah Khomeini (1900–1989)," in *BBC History*, 2012, http://www.bbc.co.uk/history/historic_figures/khome (accessed January 1, 2012).

Baena, Rosalía, "Telling a Bath-Time Story: *Haroun and the Sea of Stories* as a Modern Literary Fairy Tale," in *Journal of Commonwealth Literature*, Vol. 36, No. 2, 2001, pp. 65–76.

Ball, John Clement, "Salman Rushdie: Overview," in *Contemporary Popular Writers*, edited by Dave Mote, St. James Press, 1996, pp. 344–45.

Banville, John, "An Interview with Salman Rushdie," in *New York Review of Books*, Vol. 40, No. 5, March 4, 1993, pp. 34–36.

Blishen, Edward, Review of *Haroun and the Sea of Stories*, in *New Statesman and Society*, Vol. 3, No.

120, September 28, 1990, p. 32.

Brennan, Timothy, "Salman Rushdie," in *British Writers: Supplement 4*, edited by George Stade and Carol Howard, Scribners, 1997.

"A Brief History of the Kashmir Conflict," in *Telegraph*, September 24, 2001, http://www.telegraph.co.uk/news/1399992/A-brief-history-of-the-Kashmir-conflict.html (accessed January 2, 2012).

Donoghue, Denis, Review of *Haroun and the Sea of Stories*, in *New Republic*, Vol. 203, No. 24, December 10, 1990, pp. 37–38.

Durix, Jean-Pierre, "'The Gardener of Stories': Salman Rushdie's *Haroun and the Sea of Stories*," in *Journal of Commonwealth Literature*, Vol. 28, No. 1, 1993, pp. 114–22.

Ellerby, Janet Mason, "Fiction under Siege: Rushdie's Quest for Narrative Emancipation in *Haroun and the Sea of Stories*," in *Lion and the Unicorn*, Vol. 22, No. 2, April 1998, pp. 211–20.

Harrison, James, "Chapter 1: Biography," in *Salman Rushdie*, Twayne's English Authors Series 488, Twayne Publishers, 1992.

"Kashmir," in *New York Times*, August 10, 2011, http://topics.nytimes.com/top/news/international/cou (accessed January 1, 2012).

Keats, John, "La Belle Dame Sans Merci," The Poetry Foundation website, 2011, http://www.poetryfoundation.org/poem/173740 (accessed January 7, 2012).

König, Eva, "Between Cultural Imperialism and the Fatwa: Colonial Echoes and Postcolonial Dialogue in Salman Rushdie's *Haroun and the Sea of Stories*," in *International Fiction Review*, Vol. 33, 2006, pp. 52–63.

Merivale, Patricia, "The Telling of Lies and 'the Sea of Stories': 'Haroun,' 'Pinocchio,' and the Postcolonial Artist Parable," in *ARIEL*, Vol. 28, No. 1, January 1997, pp. 193–208.

Nelson, Davia, "Salman Rushdie and the Sea of Stories: An Interview," in *American Theatre*, Vol. 20, No. 3, March 2003, pp. 26–40.

Roberts, Daniel, "Rushdie and the Romantics: Intertextual Politics in *Haroun and the Sea of Stories*," in *ARIEL*, Vol. 38, No. 4, October 2007, pp. 123–47.

Rushdie, Salman, *Haroun and the Sea of Stories*, Penguin, 1990.

Schrobsdorff, Susanna, "Ideas: *The Hero with a Thousand Faces*," in *Time*, August 30, 2011, http://entertainment.time.com/2011/08/30/all-time-100-best-nonfiction-books/slide/the-hero-with-a-thousand-faces-by-joseph-campbell/#the-hero-with-a-thousand-faces-by-joseph-campbell (accessed January 9, 2012).

Schürer, Norbert, *Salman Rushdie's "Midnight's Children": A Reader's Guide*, Continuum, 2004, p. 10.

Sen, Suchismita, "Memory, Language and Society in Salman Rushdie's *Haroun and the Sea of*

Stories," in *Contemporary Literature*, Vol. 36, No. 4, Winter 1995, pp. 654–75.

Shakespeare, William, *The Tragedy of Macbeth*, in *The Complete Works of William Shakespeare*, Massachusetts Institute of Technology, 1993, http://shakespeare.mit.edu/macbeth/macbeth.4.1.htm (accessed January 3, 2012).

Steinberg, Sybil, Review of *Haroun and the Sea of Stories*, in *Publisher's Weekly*, Vol. 237, No. 41, October 12, 1990, p. 47.

Further Reading

Grant, Damian, *Salman Rushdie* (Writers and their Work), Northcote House Publishers, 1999.

> This brief book summarizes Rushdie's life from 1947 to 1999 and provides background information on his writings.

Gurnah, Abdulrazak, ed., *The Cambridge Companion to Salman Rushdie*, Cambridge University Press, 2007.

> This book has two major sections: the first offers thematic readings of Rushdie's novels while the second discusses Rushdie as a postcolonial writer. The book also includes a detailed chronology of Rushdie's life and a useful bibliography.

Pipes, Daniel, *The Rushdie Affair: The Novel, the Ayatollah, and the West*, 2nd ed., postscript by Koenraad Elst, Transaction Publishers, 2003.

> Pipes examines the events leading to the *fatwa* issued by the Ayatollah Khomeini upon the publication of *The Satanic Verses*. He discusses specifically why the novel was considered blasphemous and the repercussions of the *fatwa* on Rushdie's life

Rushdie, Salman, *Midnight's Children*, Knopf, 1981.

> *Midnight's Children* was Rushdie's first critical success. In 1993, it won the Booker of the Bookers award as the best Booker award winner to date. In 2008, the novel was again named the best book ever to be awarded a Booker Prize.

———, *The Wizard of Oz* (BFI Film Classics), British Film Institute, 1992.

> In this short book, Salman Rushdie provides first an essay on the famous American film followed by a short story called "The Ruby Slippers." Rushdie has claimed in many interviews that *The Wizard of Oz* was highly influential in his life, and particularly in the composition of *Haroun and the Sea of Stories*.

Teverson, Andrew, *Salman Rushdie* (Contemporary World Writers), Manchester University Press, 2008.

> Teverson provides historical, cultural, and literary contexts for Rushdie's works as well as detailed critical readings of each. He also offers a biographical section to connect Rushdie's life to his novels.

Suggested Search Terms

Salman Rushdie

Haroun and the Sea of Stories

India

Kashmir

Pakistan

Haroun and the Sea of Stories AND Magical Realism

Salman Rushdie AND the Best of the Bookers

Salman Rushdie AND storytelling

Satanic Verses

Salman Rushdie AND fatwa

Salman Rushdie AND Ayatollah Khomeini

CPSIA information can be obtained
at www.ICGtesting.com
Printed in the USA
BVHW041109110619
550700BV00018B/1110/P